A CURIOUS COLLECTION

OF
DINOSAURS

and other Prehistoric Animals

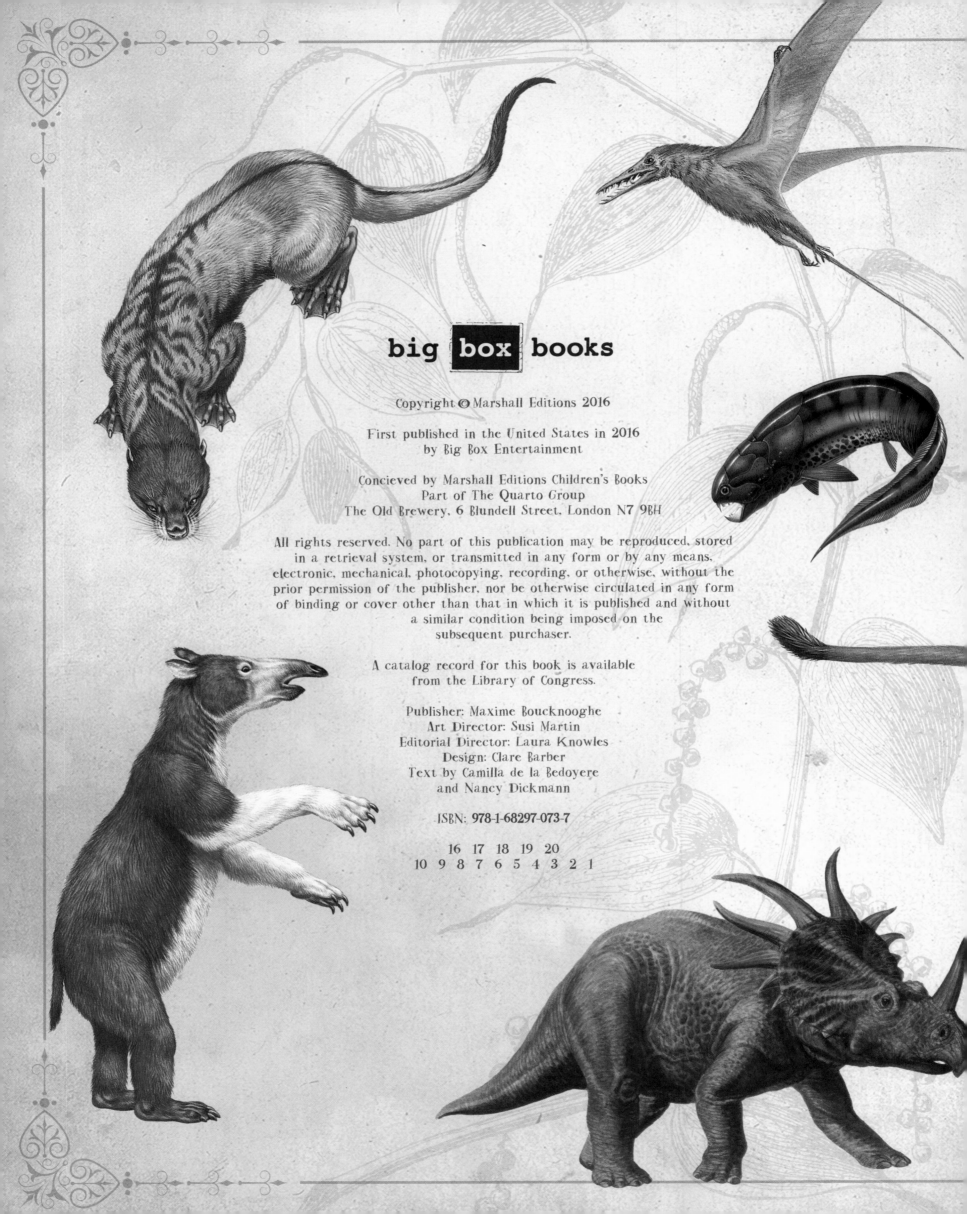

big box books

Copyright © Marshall Editions 2016

First published in the United States in 2016
by Big Box Entertainment

Concieved by Marshall Editions Children's Books
Part of The Quarto Group
The Old Brewery, 6 Blundell Street, London N7 9BH

A catalog record for this book is available
from the Library of Congress.

Publisher: Maxime Boucknooghe
Art Director: Susi Martin
Editorial Director: Laura Knowles
Design: Clare Barber
Text by Camilla de la Bedoyere
and Nancy Dickmann

ISBN: 978-1-68297-073-7

16 17 18 19 20
10 9 8 7 6 5 4 3 2 1

A CURIOUS COLLECTION
OF
DINOSAURS
and other Prehistoric Animals

big **box** books

In a time gone by...

From mighty mammoths to terrifying pteranodons, the range of creatures that have existed is truly amazing. Hundreds of millions of years ago, the animals that lived on Earth looked completely different than the ones we see today. The first animals lived in the oceans, and over millions of years they slowly evolved into reptiles, amphibians, birds, and even mammals. The most famous of these early creatures are the dinosaurs.

DRAGONFLY

LYCAENOPS

MILLERETTA

PELTOBATRACHUS

LYSTROSAURUS

TIMELINE
mya = "millions of years ago"

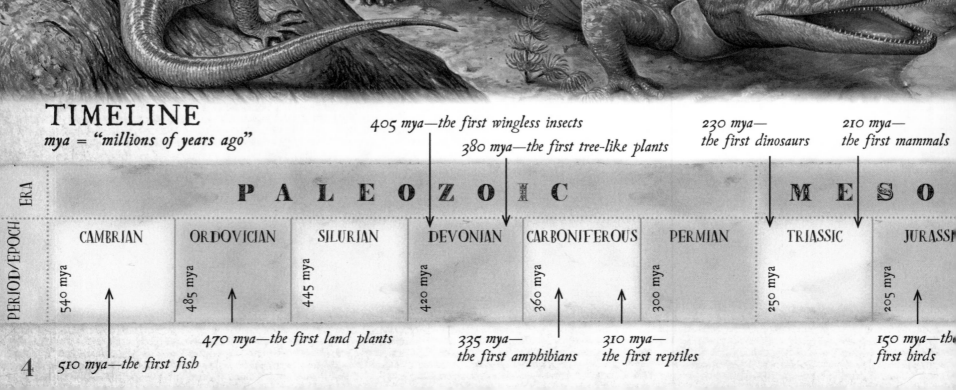

405 mya—the first wingless insects

380 mya—the first tree-like plants

230 mya—
the first dinosaurs

210 mya—
the first mammals

ERA	PALEOZOIC						MESO

PERIOD/EPOCH	CAMBRIAN	ORDOVICIAN	SILURIAN	DEVONIAN	CARBONIFEROUS	PERMIAN	TRIASSIC	JURASSI
	540 mya	485 mya	445 mya	420 mya	360 mya	300 mya	250 mya	205 mya

470 mya—the first land plants

335 mya—
the first amphibians

310 mya—
the first reptiles

150 mya—the
first birds

510 mya—the first fish

The timeline of Earth is divided into "chapters" called eras, periods, or epochs. Each of these chunks is given a name, such as "Jurassic" or "Eocene." These divisions make it easier to understand. Each animal in this book is labeled with its time period. The timeline below can show you when they lived.

I SPY

This book is full of prehistoric creatures, but hidden among them are some animals that are still alive today. Can you tell the ancient from the modern? See if you can spot the modern animal hidden in each group.

ROBERTIA

DICYNODON

PROCYNOSUCHUS

LYCAENOPS

200,000 years ago—
the first humans: Homo sapiens

Present day

IC	C E N O Z O I C						
ETACEOUS	PALEOCENE	EOCENE	OLIGOCENE	MIOCENE	PLIOCENE	PLEISTOCENE	HOLOCENE
	65 mya	55 mya	34 mya	24 mya	5 mya	2.5 mya	12,000 years ago

65 mya—mass extinction event

30 mya—the first flowering plants

Animals with Armor

Built like tanks, these armor-plated beasts appear to be fearless. Who's tough enough to take a bite?

PANOPLOSAURUS
Late Cretaceous
Pan-OP-lo-SAW-rus

Desmatosuchus looked fierce, but it was a plant eater.

STEGOSAURUS
Late Jurassic
STEG-oh-SAW-rus

DESMATOSUCHUS
Late Triassic
dez-MAT-oh-SOO-kus

Groenlandaspis was only 3 inches (7.5 cm) long, but it was an agile swimmer, using its fin-like flaps.

GROENLANDASPIS
Devonian
grohn-LAN-das-PIS

PROBOSCIS
MONKEY
Modern

CRASSIGYRINUS
Carboniferous
KRA-sig-i-RIN-us

GERROTHORAX
Late Triassic
GEH-roh-THOR-ax

Paleontologists can't agree on what this unusual horn was for!

TSINTAOSAURUS
Late Cretaceous
JING-dow-SAW-rus

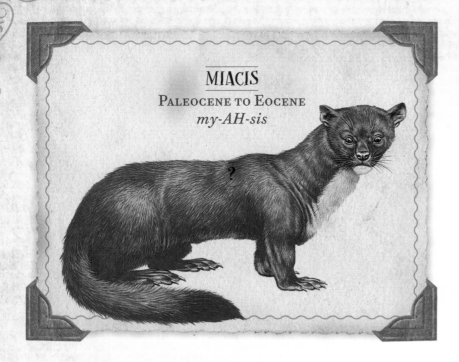

MIACIS
PALEOCENE TO EOCENE
my-AH-sis

Miacis had flexible joints that helped it scamper along tree branches as it hunted. It was only about 8 inches (20 centimeters) long.

NECROLESTES
MIOCENE
nec-ro-LES-tes

CRUSAFONTIA
EARLY CRETACEOUS
croos-a-FONT-ee-a

Mini Mammals

The first mammals lived about 200 million years ago. They were small and furry.

EUROPEAN RABBIT
MODERN

ALPHADON
Late Cretaceous to Eocene
ALF-a-don

Alphadon was an early type of marsupial, similar to the opossums and kangaroos that live today.

PTILODUS
Paleocene
til-oh-dus

ZALAMBDALESTES
Late Cretaceous
zal-am-dal-EST-es

PURGATORIUS
Paleocene
purg-a-TOR-ee-us

METACHEIROMYS
Eocene
meta-KIR-oh-mis

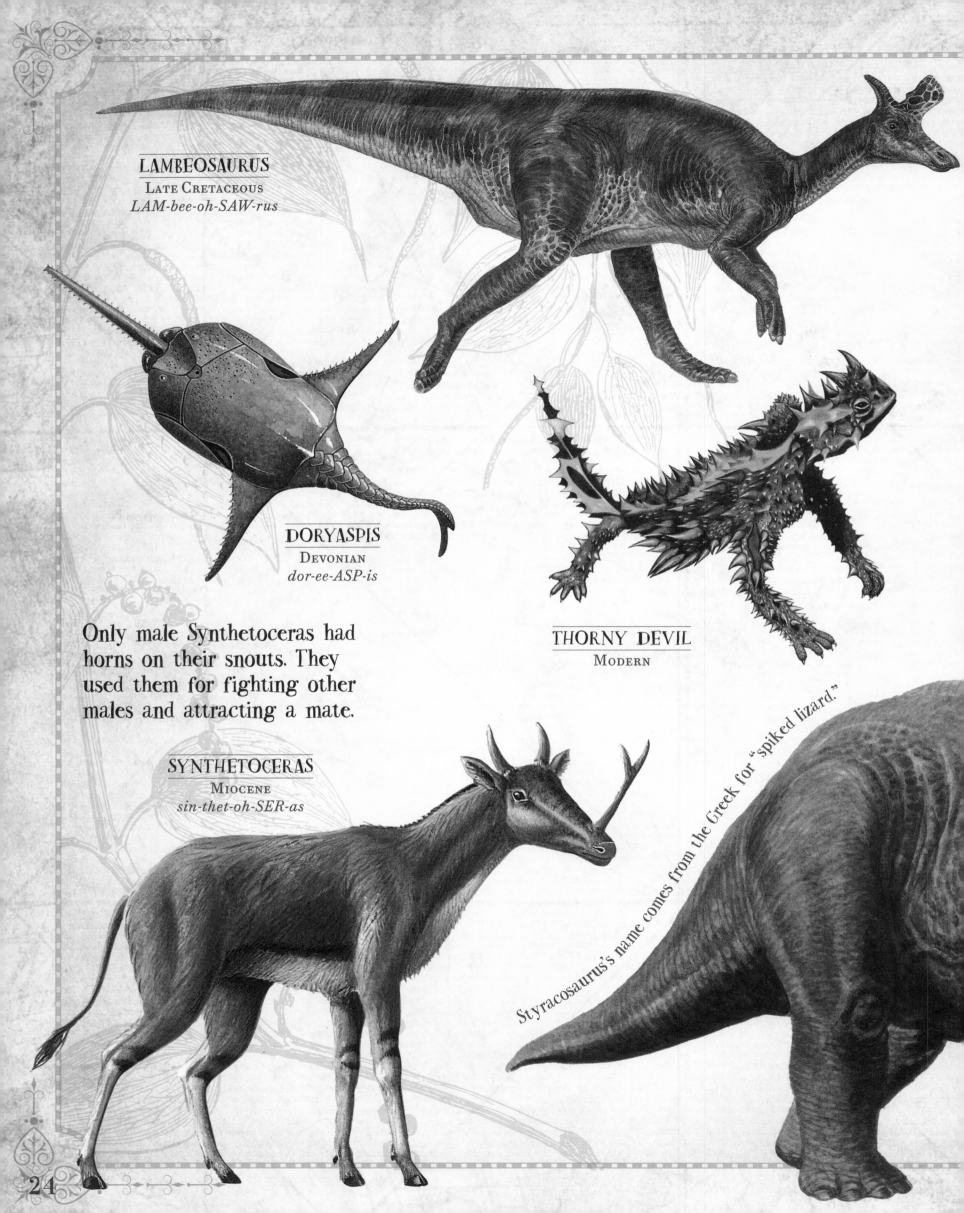

LAMBEOSAURUS
Late Cretaceous
LAM-bee-oh-SAW-rus

DORYASPIS
Devonian
dor-ee-ASP-is

THORNY DEVIL
Modern

Only male Synthetoceras had horns on their snouts. They used them for fighting other males and attracting a mate.

SYNTHETOCERAS
Miocene
sin-thet-oh-SER-as

Styracosaurus's name comes from the Greek for "spiked lizard."

Strange Spikes

These bony bumps, hard horns, and super-large scales and spikes are not just for decoration.

SCLERORHYNCHUS
Late Cretaceous
skleh-roh-RIN-kuss

Elginia looked fierce, but it was only 2 feet (60 centimeters) long and ate plants!

ELGINIA
Permian
el-GIN-ee-ah

Proganochelys was one of the earliest known turtles. Unlike modern turtles, it had teeth in its mouth.

STYRACOSAURUS
Early Cretaceous
sty-RAK-oh-SAW-rus

PROGANOCHELYS
Late Triassic
pro-gan-oh-KEEL-is

25

GREAT BLACK-BACKED GULL
Modern

ICARONYCTERIS
Eocene
ik-a-roh-NIK-ter-is

Masters of the Air

See these aerial acrobats swoop, soar, glide, flit and flap through the skies.

QUETZALCOATLUS
Late Cretaceous
ket-zal-coh-at-lus

Dimorphodon's large head looked a bit like a modern-day puffin's!

DIMORPHODON
Early Jurassic
dy-MORF-oh-don

ANUROGNATHUS
Late Jurassic
ann-yew-ro-KNAY-thus

Scientists think Dimorphodon may have caught insects in the air and on the ground.

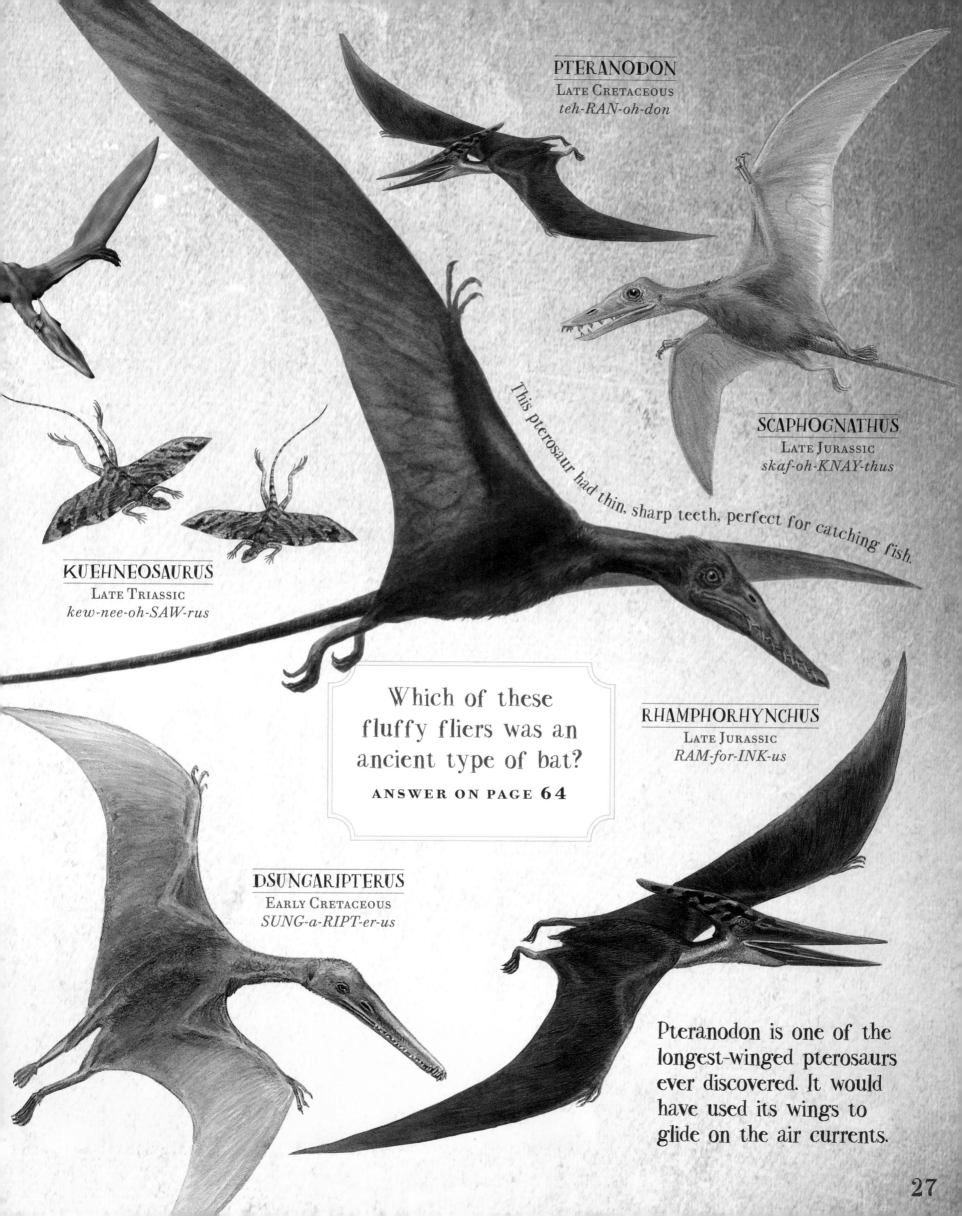

PTERANODON
Late Cretaceous
teh-RAN-oh-don

SCAPHOGNATHUS
Late Jurassic
skaf-oh-KNAY-thus

This pterosaur had thin, sharp teeth, perfect for catching fish.

KUEHNEOSAURUS
Late Triassic
kew-nee-oh-SAW-rus

Which of these
fluffy fliers was an
ancient type of bat?

ANSWER ON PAGE 64

RHAMPHORHYNCHUS
Late Jurassic
RAM-for-INK-us

DSUNGARIPTERUS
Early Cretaceous
SUNG-a-RIPT-er-us

Pteranodon is one of the
longest-winged pterosaurs
ever discovered. It would
have used its wings to
glide on the air currents.

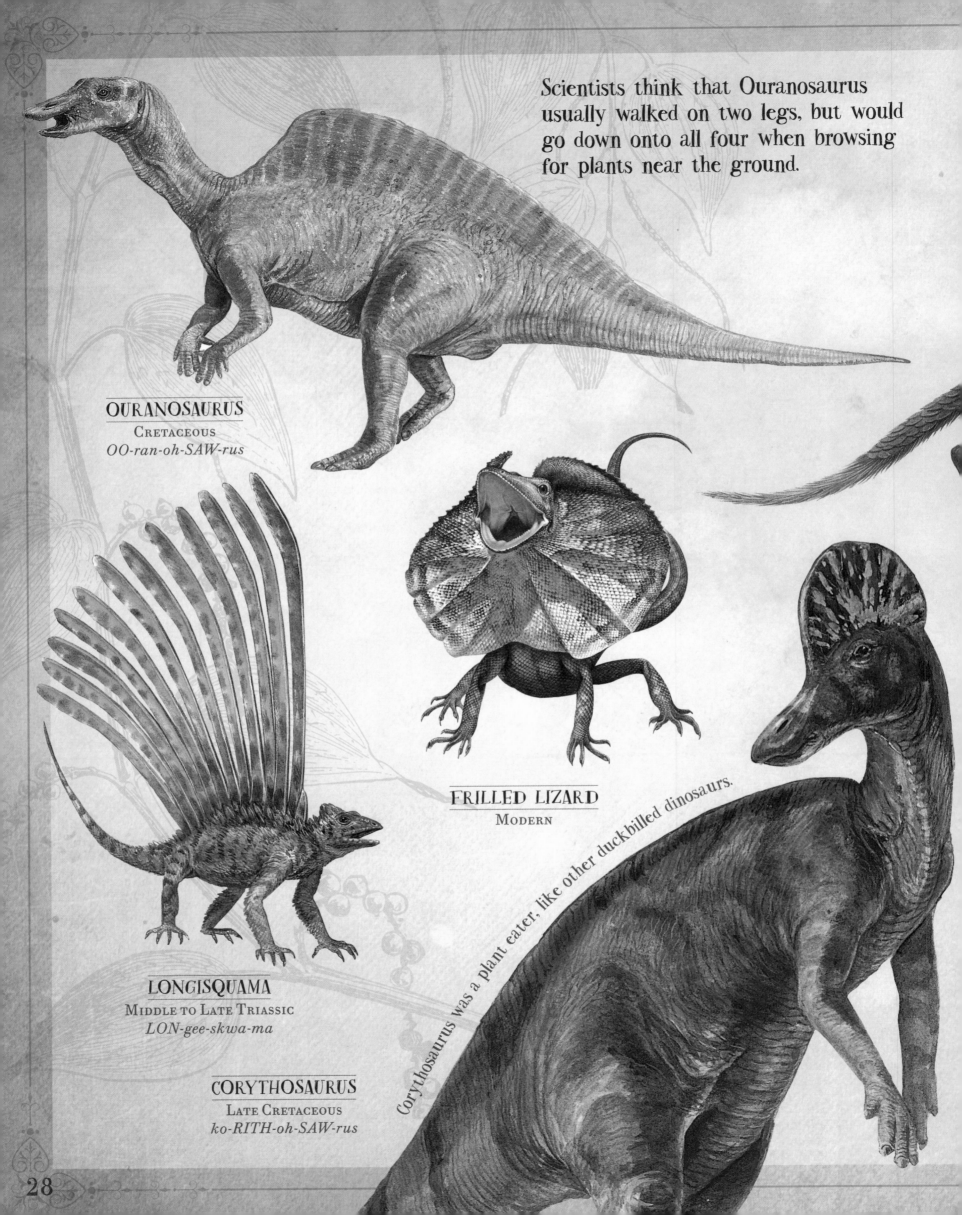

Scientists think that Ouranosaurus usually walked on two legs, but would go down onto all four when browsing for plants near the ground.

OURANOSAURUS
Cretaceous
OO-ran-oh-SAW-rus

LONGISQUAMA
Middle to Late Triassic
LON-gee-skwa-ma

CORYTHOSAURUS
Late Cretaceous
ko-RITH-oh-SAW-rus

FRILLED LIZARD
Modern

Corythosaurus was a plant eater, like other duckbilled dinosaurs.

Which of these creatures used its strange shape to keep warm?

ANSWER ON PAGE 64

This impressive crest was hollow and may have acted like a microphone.

PARASAUROLOPHUS
Late Cretaceous
PARA-saw-ROL-oh-fus

EOMANIS
Eocene
eo-MAN-is

Bizarre Bodies

Animals, from prehistory to today, come in many shapes and sizes. It takes all kinds!

DIMETRODON
Permian
di-MEE-troh-don

DIPLOCAULUS
Permian
dip-lo-KAW-lus

This amazing "fin" was made of spines up to 3 feet (1 meter) long, attached to the backbone with a sheet of skin covering them.

Terrestrisuchus was one of the first members of the crocodile family. It fed on insects and other small creatures.

TERRESTRISUCHUS
Late Triassic
ter-EST-ri-SOOK-us

PLANOCEPHALOSAURUS
Late Triassic
PLANE-oh-SEF-al-oh-SAW-rus

Coelurus was a small dinosaur, only as tall as a child.

COELURUS
Late Jurassic to Early Cretaceous
SEE-loo-rus

Hapalops is related to the sloths that live today. However, it spent more time on the ground than in trees.

HAPALOPS
Miocene
HAP-al-ops

Spots and Speckles

These beauties are gorgeous in their coats, scales, and skins of many colors.

BOROPHAGUS
Miocene to Pliocene
bo-RO-fay-gus

When stretched out, these skin flaps helped with gliding.

PLANETETHERIUM
Paleocene
PLAN-et-ee-THER-ee-um

GEMUENDINA
Devonian
JEM-oo-en-DEE-na

NORTHERN LEOPARD FROG
Modern

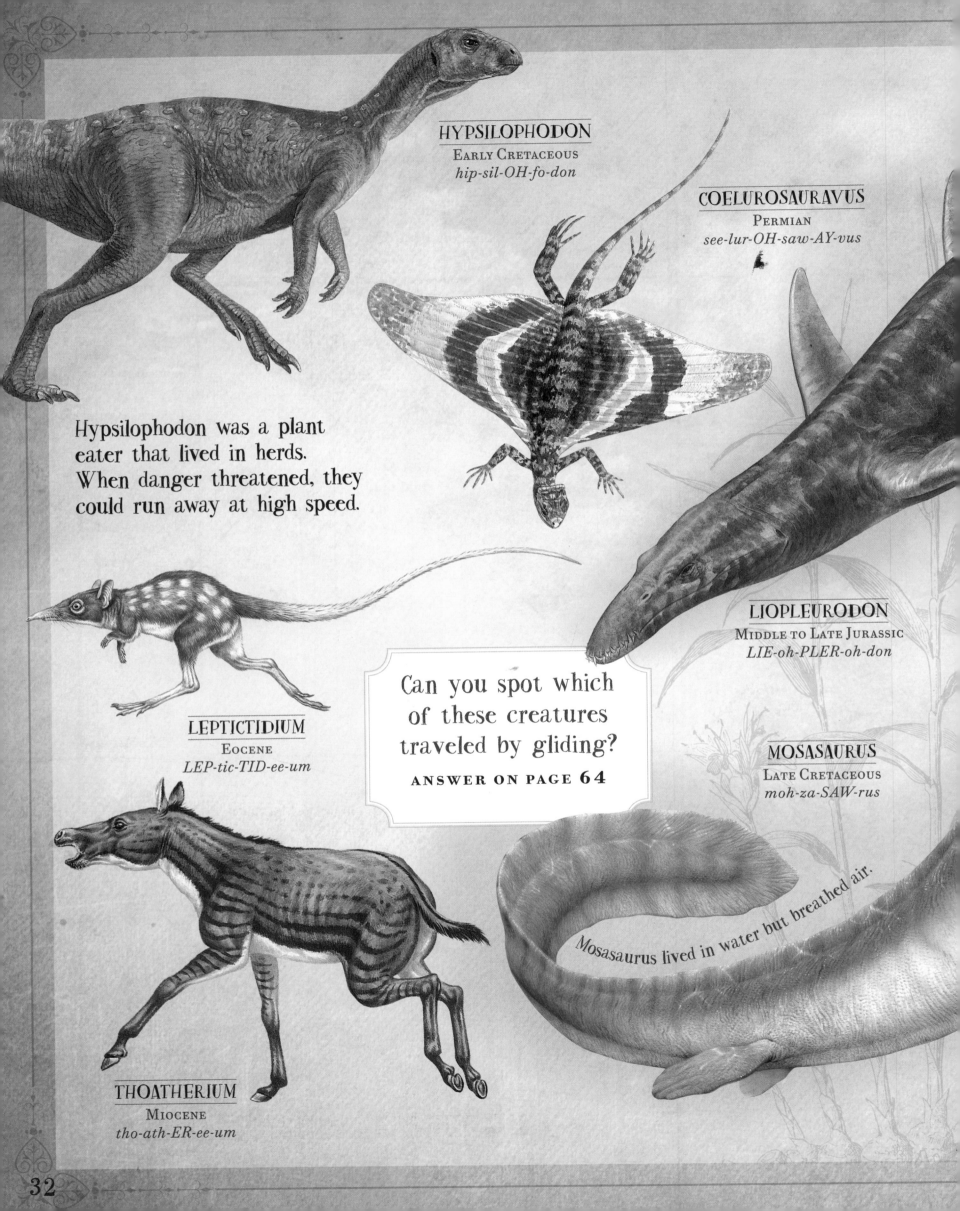

HYPSILOPHODON
EARLY CRETACEOUS
hip-sil-OH-fo-don

COELUROSAURAVUS
PERMIAN
see-lur-OH-saw-AY-vus

Hypsilophodon was a plant eater that lived in herds. When danger threatened, they could run away at high speed.

LIOPLEURODON
MIDDLE TO LATE JURASSIC
LIE-oh-PLER-oh-don

Can you spot which of these creatures traveled by gliding?

ANSWER ON PAGE 64

LEPTICTIDIUM
EOCENE
LEP-tic-TID-ee-um

MOSASAURUS
LATE CRETACEOUS
moh-za-SAW-rus

Mosasaurus lived in water but breathed air.

THOATHERIUM
MIOCENE
tho-ath-ER-ee-um

Fast Movers

Beasts need to move quickly to find food, water, shelter, and mates.

RUBY-THROATED
HUMMINGBIRD
Modern

VELOCIRAPTOR
Late Cretaceous
vel-O-si-RAP-tor

Hyracodon looked like early horses and ponies, but it was more closely related to the rhinoceros.

HYRACODON
Eocene to Oligocene
hi-RAK-oh-don

HETERODONTOSAURUS
EARLY JURASSIC
HET-er-oh-DONT-oh-SAW-rus

This tiny carnivore could run on two legs to escape danger.

EUPARKERIA
EARLY TRIASSIC
YOO-park-EE-ree-a

MASSOSPONDYLUS
LATE TRIASSIC TO EARLY JURASSIC
MASS-oh-SPOND-i-lus

Prenocephale's bony dome was surrounded by spikes and bumps. It lived in forests, where it ate plants.

PRENOCEPHALE
LATE CRETACEOUS
pren-oh-SEF-a-lee

ORNITHOSUCHUS
Late Triassic
OR-nith-oh-SOOK-us

Paleontologists think that Ornithosuchus spent most of its time on four legs, but could run on two when it needed to move more quickly.

GREAT JERBOA
Modern

Two Feet

Because of the shape of their hip bones, some beasts walk on four legs while others just use two.

Massospondylus probably used its front legs for gathering food.

SINOSAUROPTERYX
Early Cretaceous
SIGH-no-saw-OP-ter-iks

Mighty Mammoths

The most magnificent of all mammals, these are members of the elephant family.

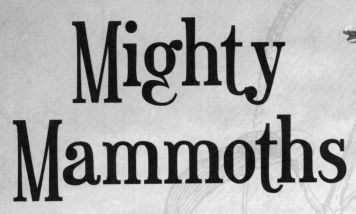

DEINOTHERIUM
MIOCENE TO EARLY PLEISTOCENE
dine-o-THER-ee-um

Moeritherium may not have had much of a trunk, but its broad, thick upper lip helped it root around for swamp plants.

MOERITHERIUM
EOCENE TO OLIGOCENE
moh-er-ee-THER-ee-um

AMEBELODON
MIOCENE
am-eh-BEL-oh-don

MAMMUTHUS MERIDIONALIS
PLEISTOCENE
ma-mu-thus mer-id-ee-on-AL-is

Deinotherium's bizarre tusks may have been used for stripping the bark from trees, or for digging up roots to eat.

Which of these giants lived in the coldest places?

ANSWER ON PAGE 64

ASIAN ELEPHANT
MODERN

The woolly mammoth lived at the same time as humans, who hunted it.

WOOLLY MAMMOTH
PLEISTOCENE TO RECENT (EXTINCT)

Nibblers and Grazers

It takes strong jaws and tough teeth to munch on grass, seeds, and nuts.

BLASTOMERYX
Oligocene to Miocene
blast-OM-er-ix

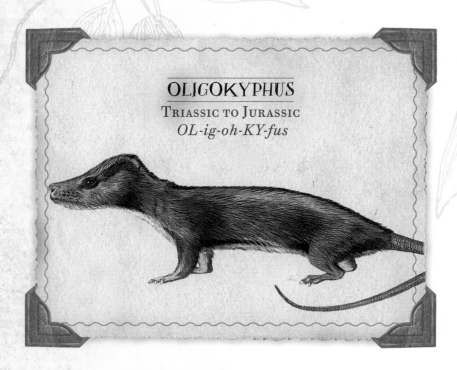

OLIGOKYPHUS
Triassic to Jurassic
OL-ig-oh-KY-fus

The nibblers shown here are all mammals. Mammals first appeared during the late Triassic, but many more types evolved after the dinosaurs died out.

ARIZONA COTTON RAT
Modern

ARGYROLAGUS
Pliocene
ar-ger-oh-LA-gus

PROTYPOTHERIUM
MIOCENE
PRO-tip-o-THER-ee-um

EOCARDIA
MIOCENE
ee-oh-CARD-ee-a

RHYNCHIPPUS
EOCENE TO
OLIGOCENE
rin-kip-us

Eocardia lived in South America and is related to modern-day guinea pigs. Can you see the resemblance?

CERATOGAULUS
MIOCENE TO PLIOCENE
SER-at-oh-GOW-lus

PALAEOLAGUS
EOCENE TO OLIGOCENE
pay-lee-oh-LA-gus

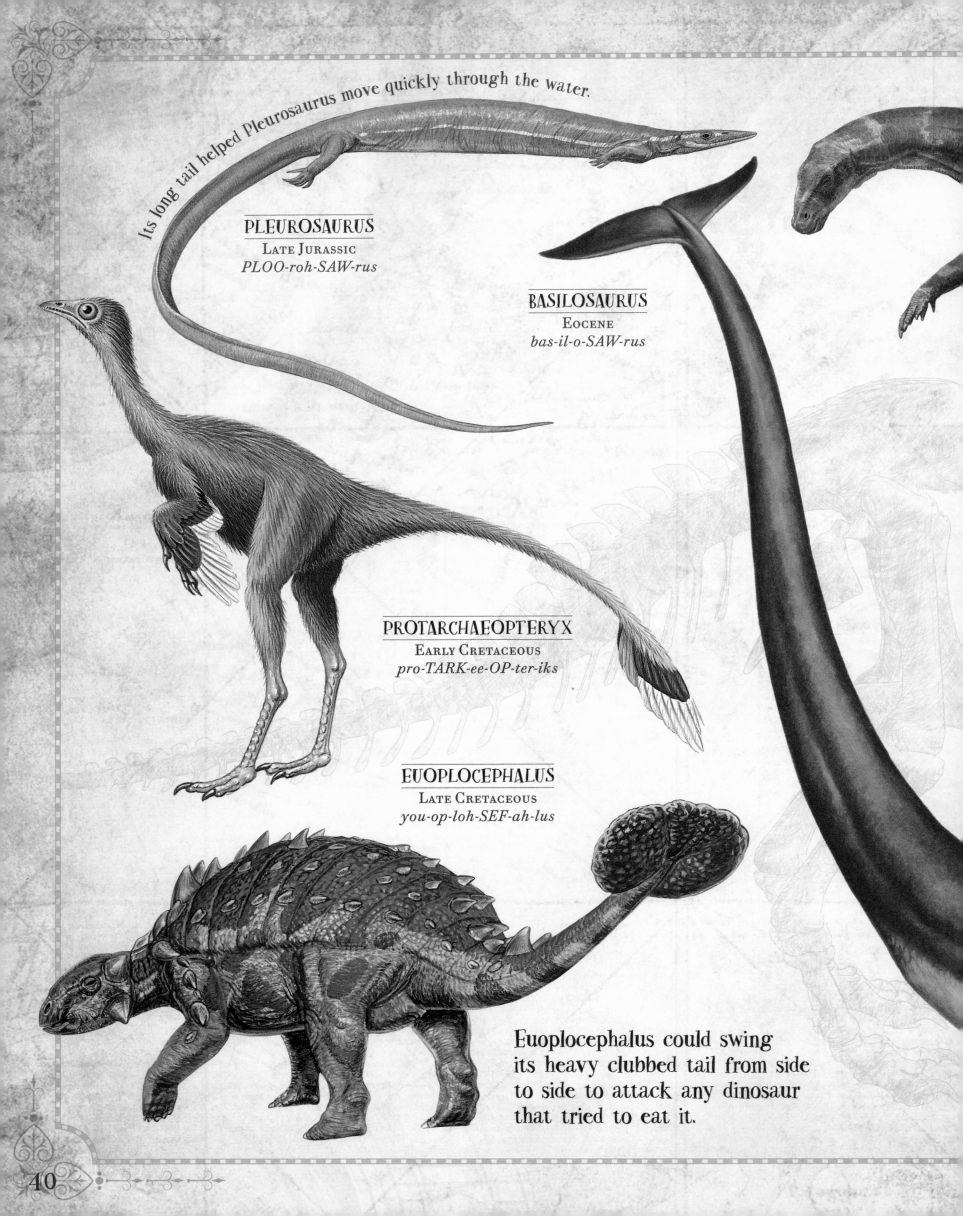

Its long tail helped Pleurosaurus move quickly through the water.

PLEUROSAURUS
Late Jurassic
PLOO-roh-SAW-rus

BASILOSAURUS
Eocene
bas-il-o-SAW-rus

PROTARCHAEOPTERYX
Early Cretaceous
pro-TARK-ee-OP-ter-iks

EUOPLOCEPHALUS
Late Cretaceous
you-op-loh-SEF-ah-lus

Euoplocephalus could swing its heavy clubbed tail from side to side to attack any dinosaur that tried to eat it.

Tenontosaurus had special tendons in its back and tail that could help hold the unusually long tail up off the ground.

Chriacus's back legs were made for climbing trees.

TENONTOSAURUS
EARLY CRETACEOUS
teh-non-to-SAW-rus

CHRIACUS
PALEOCENE
cry-ACK-us

Terrific Tails

A tail can be used for many things: balancing, swimming, and even whacking other animals!

GREATER BUSH BABY
MODERN

Incredible Hulks

When size is on your side there is little to fear. Big is beautiful!

Plateosaurus reared up on its hind legs to reach the leaves of tall trees.

PLATEOSAURUS
Late Triassic
PLAT-ee-oh-SAW-rus

Arsinoitherium was as tall as a grown man. It had a pair of massive hollow horns, with two smaller horns behind.

ARSINOITHERIUM
Eocene to Oligocene
ars-in-oy-THER-ee-um

Riojasaurus moved slowly on its four strong legs.

BRACHIOSAURUS
LATE JURASSIC
BRACK-ee-oh-SAW-rus

RIOJASAURUS
LATE TRIASSIC
ree-okah-SAW-rus

HIPPOPOTAMUS
MODERN

BARAPASAURUS
EARLY JURASSIC
ba-RA-pa-SAW-rus

The enormous Barapasaurus was one of the first dinosaurs of this type to exist. Its name means "big-legged lizard."

Slippery Skin

With slimy skin and smooth scales, these creatures are built for slipping and sliding through the weeds and reeds.

Ophiderpeton was a burrower, looking for insects, worms, centipedes, snails, and other tiny creatures to eat.

PHLEGETHONTIA
CARBONIFEROUS TO PERMIAN
FLE-geh-THON-tee-ah

PALAEOBATRACHUS
CRETACEOUS TO MIOCENE
PAY-lee-oh-ba-TRA-kus

PANTYLUS
EARLY PERMIAN
pan-TIE-lus

This lizard swam by moving its body like a snake does.

OPHIDERPETON
Carboniferous to Permian
oh-fi-DER-peh-ton

MICROBRACHIS
Carboniferous
MY-kro-BRAK-is

Microbrachis's body looks like a salamander, and like many modern salamanders, it was small—about 6 inches (15 centimeters) long.

VIERAELLA
Early Jurassic
VI-er-RAY-la

PACHYRHACHIS
Late Cretaceous
PAK-ee-RAK-iss

KARAURUS
Late Jurassic
ka-RAW-rus

Karaurus is the oldest known salamander. It was a good swimmer and fed on small invertebrates.

SPOTTED SALAMANDER
Modern

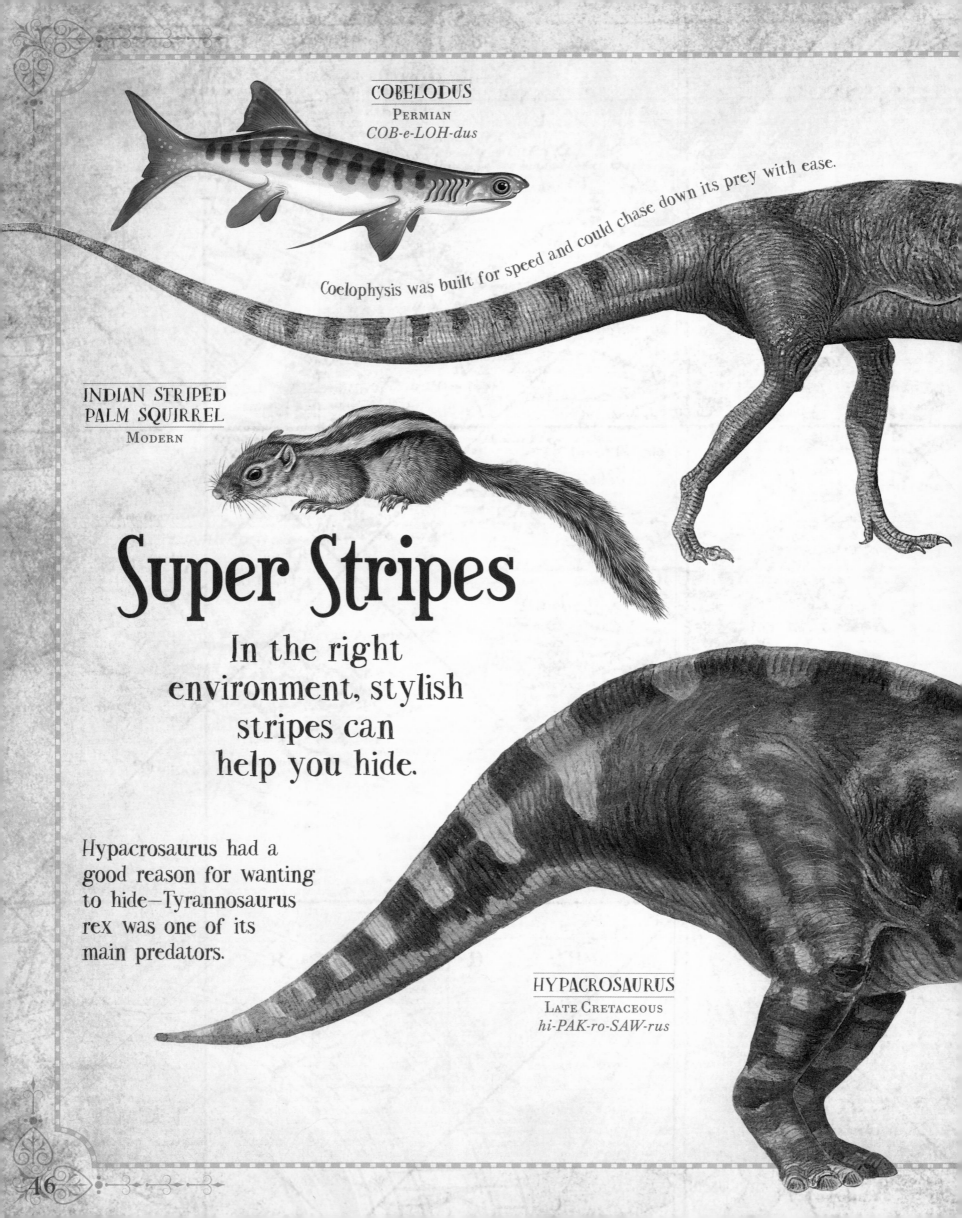

COBELODUS
Permian
COB-e-LOH-dus

Coelophysis was built for speed and could chase down its prey with ease.

INDIAN STRIPED PALM SQUIRREL
Modern

Super Stripes

In the right environment, stylish stripes can help you hide.

Hypacrosaurus had a good reason for wanting to hide—Tyrannosaurus rex was one of its main predators.

HYPACROSAURUS
Late Cretaceous
hi-PAK-ro-SAW-rus

ARCHAEOTHERIUM
Eocene to Oligocene
ARK-ee-oh-THER-ee-um

COELOPHYSIS
Triassic to Jurassic
seel-oh-FY-sis

The name "Ornithomimus" comes from the Greek for "bird mimic."

ORNITHOMIMUS
Late Cretaceous
ORN-ith-oh-MIM-us

Can you tell which
of these beasts were
hunters?

ANSWER ON PAGE 64

DIACODEXIS
Eocene
dee-a-co-DEX-is

SHONISAURUS
Late Triassic
SHOH-nee-SAW-rus

SMOOTH HAMMERHEAD
Modern

Danger Below

Underneath the rippling surface of the water, danger lurks in the form of these hungry hunters.

MACROPLATA
Early Jurassic
mac-roh-PLAT-a

Macroplata had a large skull, a long neck, and four powerful flippers to move it through the water.

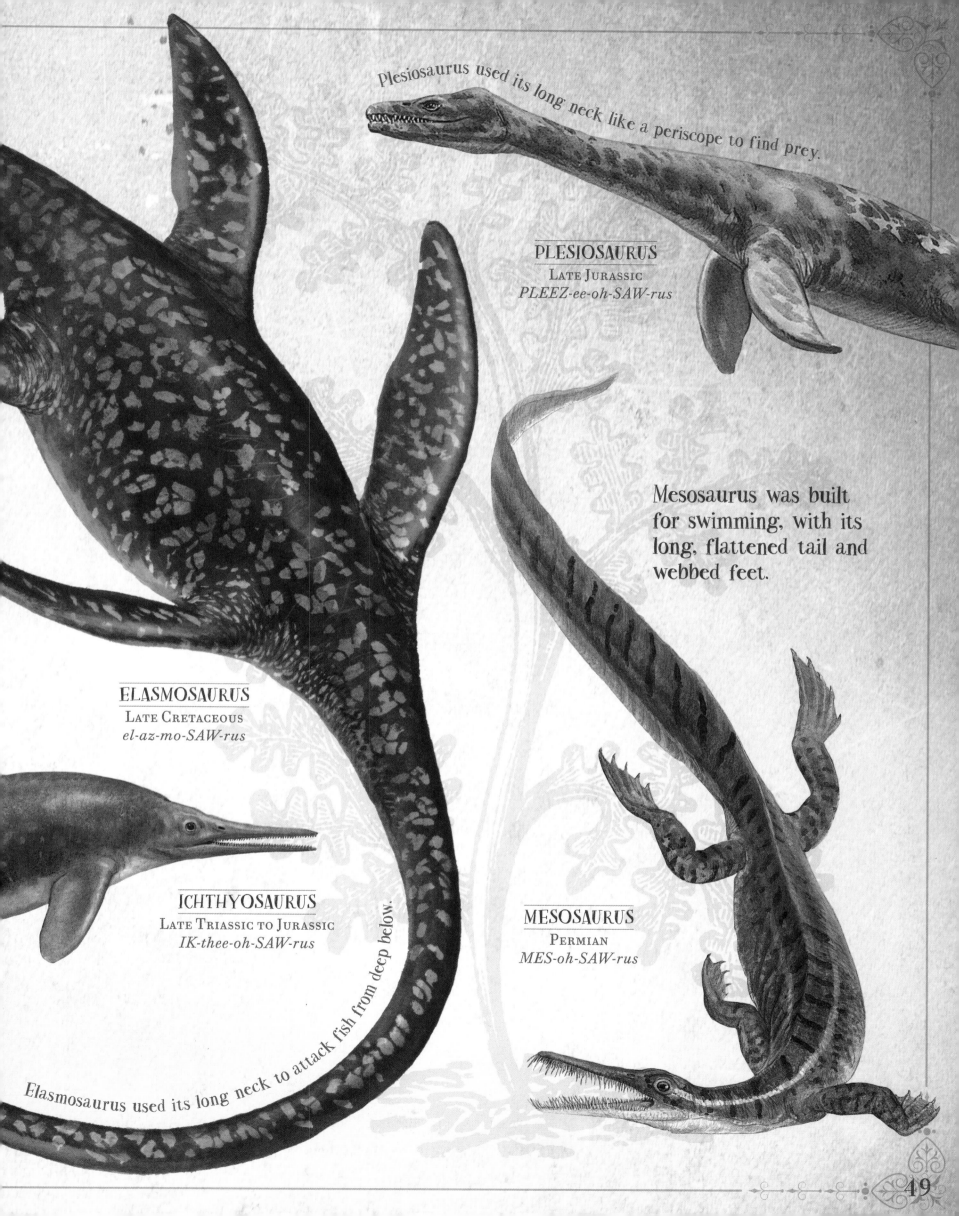

Plesiosaurus used its long neck like a periscope to find prey.

PLESIOSAURUS
Late Jurassic
PLEEZ-ee-oh-SAW-rus

Mesosaurus was built for swimming, with its long, flattened tail and webbed feet.

ELASMOSAURUS
Late Cretaceous
el-az-mo-SAW-rus

ICHTHYOSAURUS
Late Triassic to Jurassic
IK-thee-oh-SAW-rus

MESOSAURUS
Permian
MES-oh-SAW-rus

Elasmosaurus used its long neck to attack fish from deep below.

This creature's big eyes may have helped it hunt at night.

PLESICTIS
Oligocene to Miocene
ples-IK-tis

WILD YAK
Modern

Toxodon had surprisingly small feet for its size. Its front legs were shorter than the back legs.

TOXODON
Miocene to Pleistocene
TOX-o-don

Cute and Cuddly

These critters might be soft and furry, but you wouldn't want to give one a hug.